LOVE YOURSELF

The Secret Key to
Transforming Your Life

A Multimedia Enhanced Book

by Embrosewyn Tazkuvel

Published by Kaleidoscope Productions
1467 Siskiyou Boulevard, Ste. 9
Ashland, OR 97520
www.kaleidoscope-publications.com

Cover design & book layout by Sumara Elan Love
www.3wizardz.com

ISBN 978-0-938001-04-1

~♥~

CONTENTS

~❤~

INTRODUCTION

Loving yourself is all about energy. As humans we devote a great deal of our energy through our time, thoughts and emotions to love. We read about it, watch movies and shows about it, dream about it, hope for it to bless our lives, feel like something critically important is lacking when it doesn't, and at the very least keep a sharp eye out for it when it is missing.

Too often we look to someone else to fulfill our love and crash and burn when relationships end, or fail to live up to our fantasies of what we thought they should be. When we seek love from another person or source greater than the love we give to ourselves, we set ourselves up for an inevitable hard landing when the other person or source ceases to provide the level of fulfillment we desire.

Loving yourself is a precious gift from you to you. It is an incredibly powerful energy that not only enhances your ability to give love more fully to others, it also creates a positive energy of expanding reverberation that brings more love, friendship and appreciation to you from all directions. It is the inner light that illuminates your life empowering you to create the kind of life you desire and dream.

The relationship you have with yourself is the most important one in your life. Happiness will forever be fleeting if you do not have peace, respect and love for yourself. It's not selfish. It's not vain. It is in fact the key to transforming your life. Inward reflection and appreciation will open up clearer channels to God and the divine. Relationships with everyone else will be enhanced as your relationship with yourself expands and is uplifted. All other relationships are only mirrors of the one you have within. As you love yourself, are kind to yourself, respect yourself, so too will you be able to give those and so many other good qualities to others in equal measure to that which you give to yourself.

This is a very special book to help you discover your inner glow of love. It's actually short on words. Many great writers and self-help teachers have spoken eloquently and at great length on the subject already. What you will find within the covers of this book are two great keys you will find no other place. These two keys will proactively bring you to the serenity of self-love regardless of whether you are currently near or far from that place of peace.

Are you familiar with the infinity symbol? It looks pretty much like the number 8 turned on its side. As love for yourself should be now and forever, in this book you will find 88 reasons why loving yourself is vitally important to your happiness, personal growth and expansion, and the happiness of everyone whose lives you touch. Most people would be surprised there could be a list that long just about loving yourself! But with each short phrase you read your mind begins to understand in greater depth how important loving yourself is for all aspects of your life and relationships. As your mind understands, your life follows.

Lastly, this book leaves you with a gift. Inside you'll find two short, but very valuable multimedia flash presentations. One is entitled *Forgive Yourself*. The other is *Love Yourself*. These are not normal flash presentations. They are self-hypnosis, positive affirmations that will rapidly help you achieve greater self-love and more fulfilling love-filled realities in your life. As soft repetitive music plays in the background, images reinforcing the theme of loving yourself will flash by on your screen about three per second, accompanied by short phrases at the top of the image. In a quick 7-10 minute session, sitting at

Love Yourself

home in front of your computer, you will find the flash presentations buoy and motivate you. Repeat them twice a day for several days and you will find they are transformative.

~♥~

THE MAGIC OF LOVE

Have you ever wished to have magical powers and abilities? Have you ever dreamed of being able to utter a secret phrase, wave your hand or point your wand and be able to transform the ordinary into the extraordinary? In reality you do have these great powers. You can rapidly transform your life, enhance your relationships, increase your financial success, improve your physical appearance, excel in school, and gain a zest and enthusiasm for living. The metamorphosis begins simply by looking at yourself in the mirror and saying aloud one of the most magical incantations ever spoken upon the Earth ~ *I love you.* Though that is only the first step, it is so essential that without love for yourself all endeavors become dreary and burdensome, if not impossible. Loving yourself is the secret key to transforming your life.

On first thought it may seem that saying *I love you* to yourself is rather vain, tending to lead to subsequent actions that would manifest with conceit. And such lofty thoughts of oneself, if not grounded in gratitude and tempered by life challenges, certainly can and does lead to boorish arrogance with some people.

Then there are all the scenarios where it would seem to many to be ludicrous for people to feel they love themselves. The long-term unemployed Dad looks in the mirror and thinks, "I'm a failure." The overweight Mom looks in the mirror hating her body, screaming silently to herself, "I'm fat!" The 75 year old widowed grandmother who should have retired years ago, but still needs to struggle at a minimum wage job to pay her bills, looks in the mirror and thinks, "I'm not a has been, I'm a never been." The divorced father of three, who longs to see his children living on the other side of the country with his divorced wife, looks in the mirror and thinks, "Does my life have a purpose anymore?"

Due to either feelings of low self-esteem or the opinion that loving yourself would be vain and conceited, many people simply cannot look themselves in the mirror, even if alone in their room, and say out loud, *I love you* with honest sincerity. In seminars I've held I've asked people in attendance, most who outwardly seem balanced, fit and happy, to hold up a mirror, look themselves in the eyes in the mirror and simply say out loud, *I love you.* Without exception, about a third of the participants simply could not do it. They just couldn't get the words to come out of their mouth. Another third would speak the words, but would render them meaningless by laughing as they said them, or exaggerating their delivery as if they were actors in a play, or gritting their teeth and struggling with themselves as they forced them out. Usually only about one third of the participants could look at themselves in a mirror and say *I love you*, in a calm voice with humble sincerity and ease.

Some seminar participants voiced alternatives such as "I accept myself," or "I like myself just the way I am." But there is no magic in those phrases; there is no special transformative power in those positive but still half-baked phrases.

If you are married or in a long-term relationship or ever have been, think about how you feel and how your partner feels, when you gently hold their hand, earnestly look into their eyes, and tenderly tell them *I love you* from the depths of your heart. Now think how less deep your feelings for them and theirs for you would be, if instead you told them, "I accept you", or "I like you just the way you are." Though those are still positive words, they have only a transitory, skin-deep effect. It is only the great word of power "love" and that word alone, that has the magical ability to enter into every fiber of your being, filling you with endless hope and unbound joy, empowering you to leap chasms greater than you believed you could leap.

The power of *I love you* is just as powerful said aloud while looking at yourself in the mirror, as it is voiced with passion to another person that you love with deep and profound affection and commitment. Only in the case of you and the mirror, the great transformation to a new reality, the magic that overcomes all barriers, the power of love, begins to stir inside of you!

Returning to the earlier examples of people like the overweight woman or the unemployed man, many people feel so bad about some or all aspects of themselves that it seems impossible to them to look in the mirror and voice *I love you* out loud. But if you want the magic you must say the magical word and say it often. As great a challenge as that may be, it is an essential first step to transforming every aspect of your life to a better state of being. Even if you must say the words through gritted teeth, forcing them out one by one, so let it be. The words *I love you* truly are magical and they will begin to work their enchantment little by little, every time that you say them.

~♥~

WHY IS LOVE SO POWERFUL?

How can this be? How can words that seem repugnant for some people to say to themselves actually have not just a good effect, but eventually a glorious one? It is because "love" is the single emotion and state of mind that embodies your whole being and does not dissipate with time. When you love someone, be it a parent, a child, or a lover, the moments in time that you loved them are forever. Every second you loved them is irreversibly etched into your cells, forged on the shared experiences, common interests, nurtured relationship, and resonance of personalities and desires that created the love.

Even when love is broken, and a relationship ends, a part of your heart still remains with the lost love in the memories of the moments when it was good and not lost, despite all the anger and upset you may feel at the moment. Relationships diverge, individuals change and couples sometimes grow separately on divergent paths. Resonance that was, may become a dissonance that can no longer be tolerated. But the joyous shared moments in your life that created the love always remain inside of you, even when tamped down very deep, the wondrous moments of days gone by, even if only fleetingly short, never vanish completely. That is why love is such powerful magic.

Love calls to each of us. It beckons to us from our deepest, most primal self. Love is ambrosia for the soul that satisfies and nourishes us, empowers us more than any other thing we can eat, drink, read, think, feel or experience. It calls and you are compelled to answer. Despite any and all obstacles that may stand in your way, despite all of your personal baggage weighing you down, whatever it may be, despite whatever external or self-imposed burdens you maybe bearing, you need to answer.

~♥~

FIRST STEPS

To harness the magic power of love in your life, you must affirm love for yourself everyday in a sincere and grateful way, and do it often in multiple ways, until it has become an uneraseable part of your being. Even if there are huge parts of yourself that you don't like, maybe even hate ~ perhaps the way you look, too much weight, vile habits, or a mistake you made in the past that has had painful consequences. Any reason you have to dislike or even hate yourself needs to be set aside. Not forgotten; you will work on self-improvement and righting wrongs as you grow and progress. But the first step toward a new you begins with looking yourself in the mirror and saying aloud *I love you.*

Perhaps you already can look at yourself and say *I love you.* Congratulations! Now say it some more.

Perhaps you have never been able to say it. It doesn't matter. Say it now, even if it comes out in a whisper or through gritted teeth.

Repetition is part of the magic. You are constructing the magnificent edifice of your future. Every time you affirm that you love yourself you are adding another floor to your personal skyscraper. The more you affirm *I love you* to yourself, the more your brain accepts that reality. When your mind is invested in the reality of a grateful, humble love for yourself, it releases hormones and endorphins that buoy your moods, increase your self-confidence and make you excited about even mundane tasks in your life. Then when you are hit by one of life's occasional trucks of setback or disappointment, it becomes much easier to get back up, brush off the dust and carry on.

Best of all, love yourself and life loves you back! It's like a mirror; the energy that you put out comes back to you from all directions, from the people you know to the situations and opportunities you encounter in life. You'll actually be hit by far fewer trucks when a humble love for yourself is nurtured in your heart.

~♥~

IN A RUT?

In Og Mandino's famous book, *The Greatest Salesman in the World,* he pointed out that to permanently improve yourself you cannot simply try to give up old bad habits. Og concluded that we are all slaves to our habits. Whether they are good habits or bad habits, we continue to do them habitually. The lead character in his book made the commitment to replace the old unhelpful habits with new and better habits by stating to himself, "if I must be a slave to habits, let me be a slave to good habits." He confirmed the only successful way to be rid of bad habits was to replace them with better ones, "only a habit can subdue another habit."

If you are not truly loving yourself, for whatever reason, you are traveling on a deeply rutted path that is taking you nowhere ~ a destructive habit of no self-love. It's a difficult rut to get out of because the path is so worn it just keeps pulling you back. The key to success is to pivot and look off the track you have been on. See the track of loving yourself that you want to be on and all the good things that come with it and go for it. Go for it with full commitment and gusto!

As you do, you will be creating a new habit, a loving yourself habit. You will be creating a new grooved path, but it's a groove you have chosen to be on. Every day, in every way that you affirm and confirm that you love yourself, your new and better habit will become stronger, the groove in your new path deeper, until suddenly before you realize it, your new habit of self-love is empowering and propelling you. It becomes your new way of thinking and your new persona.

~♥~

88 REASONS TO LOVE YOURSELF

Why should you love yourself? Well let's see ~ happier, healthier, more successful, greater fulfillment in relationships... The list is actually quite long. Here are 88 wonderful reasons to love yourself from the twenty-second step of my book *22 Steps to the Light of Your Soul*. The profound truth you will realize as you read the 88 reasons that follow, is that in loving yourself, not only are you happier and more fulfilled, but you are a blessing to everyone whose lives you touch. The whole world becomes a better place for you and everyone, by the simple commitment to love yourself.

1. Love yourself enough to love yourself; for your capacity to give love to others is only as great as your willingness to cede it to yourself.

2. Love yourself enough to **use common sense**; for a momentary thoughtless choice can bring

a lifetime of grief, even as well considered actions can grant you a lifetime of peace and happiness.

3. Love yourself enough to **be true to yourself**; that you may always be guided to paths that will expand and delight you.

4. Love yourself enough to **have faith**; for it is the power by which you may accomplish all things.

5. Love yourself enough to **be honest with yourself**; that you may have a firm foundation to achieve your dreams.

6. Love yourself enough to **develop and use your mind**; for knowledge is freedom.

7. Love yourself enough to **hold optimism within your heart and thoughts**; for it lessens the sting of every trial and lays the foundation to vanquish every obstacle.

8. Love yourself enough to **be flexible and open to change**; for it is the only certain thing in life and to attempt to deny it is to stagnate.

9. Love yourself enough to **play with laughter and spontaneity**; that your inner child of yesteryear may ever live on, lighting your

present with joy and smiles.

10. Love yourself enough to **work**; for in a worthy endeavor, by the sweat of your brow and the ingenuity of your mind, you create the future and sustain the present.

11. Love yourself enough to **ask for help when you need it and render it when you are asked**; for in asking, you edify those who selflessly render aid, and in assisting, you pass on a reciprocal energy that ripples into many lives.

12. Love yourself enough to **forgive and forget**; that you may release yourself to live anew.

13. Love yourself enough to **be a good steward**; for all that sustains your life is a gift of the Earth and the world you leave your children, for better or worse, is in your hands.

14. Love yourself enough to **stand back when pushed to the brink**; for there never was a heated moment that was not regretted, nor a cooler one that didn't offer a better choice.

15. Love yourself enough to **have a vision for the future**; for without it there is only existence and with it there is hope and inspiration.

16. Love yourself enough to **have passion**; for it

enlivens you with positive energy and a natural euphoric fulfillment.

17. Love yourself enough to **be gently quiet**; that you may hear the wisdom of others, see the beauty that surrounds you and have time to reflect upon the gems of your journey.

18. Love yourself enough to **be daring**; for only those willing to venture beyond the shore can discover new worlds.

19. Love yourself enough to **laugh, especially at yourself**: for it eases the pains of life and helps to keep molehills from becoming mountains.

20. Love yourself enough to **treat your body like a temple inside and out**; that it may bless you with physical health and mental clarity, adorn you in gracious beauty and give you the boundless energy and fortuitous longevity to experience life to the fullest.

21. Love yourself enough to **begin every venture with a positive attitude**; for the hills to climb will appear smaller and the victor's peak will arrive quicker.

22. Love yourself enough to **avoid dwelling in the past**; for when you look too long back

at yesterday you miss all the wondrous joys abounding around you today.

23. Love yourself enough to **find a positive in every negative**; for all of life is a school and every experience a lesson.

24. Love yourself enough to **live up to your highest vision**; for when you expect great things, you lay the foundation to build your tower to the sky.

25. Love yourself enough to **give additional effort**; for those willing to run an extra mile will wear the winner's crown.

26. Love yourself enough to **do a good deed every day**; for the smallest kindness to others is greater than the most illustrious of intentions.

27. Love yourself enough to **help others reach their dreams**; for the lift you give them raises you as well and in their fulfillment you find your own.

28. Love yourself enough to **accept that you are not perfect**; and that your best effort is a worthy victory.

29. Love yourself enough to **discover and connect to your inner core**; for only when you

see yourself as you really are can you find the path that leads to who you can be.

30. Love yourself enough to **refuse to falter because of failures**; for your unfulfilled victories wait for you still, if you will but finish the race.

31. Love yourself enough to have the **moral courage to speak up when injustices are committed against others**; for in silence you are an accomplice and in voice justice resounds far beyond the space in which you stand.

32. Love yourself enough to **cultivate balance in your essence**; that you may stand steady when the path is tumultuous and be able to safely pass over the yawing pitfalls of life.

33. Love yourself enough to **embrace challenges as a regular part of life**; for only when you are tested do you gain the strength to grow and expand.

34. Love yourself enough to **dream**; for only upon their sparkling wings can you soar above the clutter and see the magnificence that awaits you in the distance.

35. Love yourself enough to **admire the**

beauty and grandeur of nature; for its quiet wonder sings a soothing song of peace and an enlivening melody of hope.

36. Love yourself enough to **weep**; for every tear that falls purges your heart of poison and when you lift your head you can see the brilliant, new sun of promise through the mist.

37. Love yourself enough to give **respect and courtesy to others**; for it is the basic foundation of all beneficial, reciprocal relationships.

38. Love yourself enough to **fulfill your responsibilities**; for the trust you gain from others is more precious than gold and you lay the enduring foundation for your own self-worth.

39. Love yourself enough to be s**piritually and energetically connected to all that exists**; for when you feel the pulse of oneness in all things, it is easy to love the Earth and everyone upon it, for you are only cherishing an essential part of yourself.

40. Love yourself enough to **keep an open mind**; for a closed vessel will stagnate in its own waste and in openness you will find answers to riddles you could not fathom.

41. Love yourself enough to **avoid criticizing others**; for you only demean yourself and a kind word instead will lift you both to a higher plateau.

42. Love yourself enough to **repent and ask forgiveness**; for to ere is inescapable and hiding the wrong will only be self-destructive. The forgiveness you merit will become a hallowed remembrance, allowing forgiveness of others when they have trespassed against you.

43. Love yourself enough to **love and be loved**; for it taps an emotional well that enlivens every fiber of your being and fulfills every longing of your heart.

44. Love yourself enough to **reflect and be introspective**; for only when you gaze deeply into the labyrinth of your heart and mind can you realistically understand your strengths and weaknesses, assess how far you have come, crystallize where you want to go and formulate the best way to get there.

45. Love yourself enough to **keep an open heart**; for to lock your emotional door is to imprison yourself and turn away from the sweetness of happiness and joy.

46. Love yourself enough to **focus**; for your efforts are magnified and the fires of success burn bright only with an undistracted beam of effort that holds unwaveringly to your goal.

47. Love yourself enough to **be friendly**; for it is an elixir that sweetens the sourest dispositions, endearing friends and disarming adversaries.

48. Love yourself enough to **gain knowledge**; for ignorance is a path to mediocrity while knowledge is the portal to making dreams come true.

49. Love yourself enough to **refuse to gossip**; for to speak ill of another behind their back while smiling courteously in their presence, is to dig a two-faced morass of pettiness into which you to will one day fall without pity.

50. Love yourself enough to be **artistically creative**; for it is an ability that dwells within everyone and nurturing it into fullness unleashes a host of other talents that would have otherwise lain unknown and undiscovered.

51. Love yourself enough to **slow down and relax**; for what is the purpose of toil if you never have time to enjoy life?

52. Love yourself enough to show **sincere appreciation**; for your kind words are a balm of joy and an affirmation of pride that brings smiles and light even on the darkest day.

53. Love yourself enough to **meditate**; for it stills your restless mind and calms your anxious heart, bringing you revitalized into a new day.

54. Love yourself enough to be **kind to animals**; for the timber of your character is bared in its true form by the demonstrations of how you treat those who are defenseless before you.

55. Love yourself enough to **honor uplifting traditions**; for they are the memories of tomorrow, bequeathed in yesterday and savored today.

56. Love yourself enough to **be engaged in charitable causes**; for in selfless service to others you earn a measure of humility and a reward of gratitude greater than any monetary compensation.

57. Love yourself enough to **persevere in your endeavors**; for success waits around the next bend for the stalwart champions who stay the course till the end.

58. Love yourself enough to **get a good night's sleep**; for in your long, restful slumber you lay the foundation for a morrow that is fresher and fuller.

59. Love yourself enough to **give of your time**; for it is a most precious finite treasure, a true gift, valued greatly by all with whom you share it.

60. Love yourself enough to **do your best today**; for nothing less is worthy of you. Tomorrow is the day reserved for that which may never be, while today's victory merely awaits your resolve.

61. Love yourself enough to **cultivate a good disposition**; for you are planting a garden of civility that will spread sunshine and joy to all who partake of your company.

62. Love yourself enough to **be a peace maker**; for within an aura of respectful, reasoned, resolve, the damaging animosity of antagonists can be turned into a boon of mutual reward.

63. Love yourself enough to **speak and act positively**; for your living sunshine brightens any day and sets in motion the energies necessary to accomplish all your desires.

64. Love yourself enough to **hold serenity at the center of your being**; for when the waters of peace wash over your soul the fiery darts of life fizzle into harmless wisps of insignificance that cannot pierce you.

65. Love yourself enough to **avoid blaming others for your problems**; for deflecting cause to another merely delays correcting the flaws within yourself that allowed the problem to manifest.

66. Love yourself enough to **never hate others**; for every minute wasted in hatred is a minute lost from your life, a frittering away of time to have joy in exchange for a wrenching pit of perpetual emptiness.

67. Love yourself enough to **let go of guilt**; for everyone makes mistakes. Make amends to those wronged and within yourself, then go forward with a good heart, in forgiveness and forgetfulness, or the recriminations from the past will always present a ghostly door barring your entry to the future.

68. Love yourself enough to **have relationships with equal energy exchanges**; for as the bee takes pollen from the flower which is in turn

reproduced because of the bee, so too the health of your self-esteem calls for reciprocation in some form of equal measure to those who benefit you and avoidance of those who do not give you the same consideration.

69. Love yourself enough to **abandon anger residing within you**; for the fire of rage you stoke will burn you the most.

70. Love yourself enough to **love life even with all its challenges and imperfections**; for it gives you the opportunity to learn and grow, to love and find happiness and to leave the world better than you found it.

71. Love yourself enough to **be refreshed by new things**; for the lake of your life will stagnate and dry up unless it is continually invigorated by the stimulating inflow of fresh experiences and new knowledge.

72. Love yourself enough to **help others with their grief**; for the empathy and sympathy you give is a balm of solace that enriches you in the giving and opens you to receiving a gift that you too will someday need.

73. Love yourself enough to **rid your life of stress**; for it is a merciless foe that chips away at

your vitality, robbing you of precious years of life and many moments of happiness.

74. Love yourself enough to **love and honor nature in all of its forms**; for it is a refuge of serenity, bestowing light, warmth, beauty and sustenance; asking only that you faithfully keep it healthy and vibrant that it may ever be there to provide refreshing abundance for you and your posterity.

75. Love yourself enough to **simplify your life**; for with every superfluous layer you strip away you add resounding depth and luster.

76. Love yourself enough to **flow to your own rhythm**, for you will be more fulfilled in an hour paced by your own inner pulse, than you will ever be trying to abide by someone else's cadence.

77. Love yourself enough to **be a good example**; for by your actions many with whom you associate are also judged, and by the uprightness of your deeds you open the door to others who may be seeking the light.

78. Love yourself enough to **have no place for worry in your heart or mind**; for during the time wasted in concern about circumstances

that may never be, things that are tangible and in your hand may become neglected and lost.

79. Love yourself enough to **tell the truth**; for lies come back to bite you; they dampen your inner light with every one you tell, while your honesty is a firm foundation upon which friends and associates will confidently trust.

80. Love yourself enough to **refrain from judging others**; for to mete out criticism by thought or action, simply because another's personal choices in life are different than yours, is to allow the pettiest of character traits to hold sway over the noblest.

81. Love yourself enough to **create a sacred space in or near your home**; for you will find restful tranquility and lucid answers in a hallowed sanctuary where you can forget the world and commune in thoughtfulness with your higher self and the divine energies of the universe that smile upon you.

82. Love yourself enough to **communicate thoughtfully and clearly**; for both the written and spoken word have the power to burn or heal, anger or motivate, crush or uplift.

83. Love yourself enough to **be enthusiastic**; for

it is the spark that creates bonfires of success, impels others to greater efforts and snatches victory from defeat.

84. Love yourself enough to **be sincerely interested in other people**; for to learn all they have to teach you from their lives, you must take the time to earnestly listen to their experiences and wisdom.

85. Love yourself enough to **create a legacy that will outlast you**; that your stature may grow with your foresight and the good light of your life may continue to spread sunshine upon the world, enriching the lives of generations to come.

86. Love yourself enough to **honor your truth and walk your talk**; for your noble words and beliefs are as worthless as dust upon the desert wind unless you give them substance and meaning by living your ideals everyday.

87. Love yourself enough to **seek out and find God**, for your immutable connection to something greater will always beckon and you will only find the fullness you seek once you heed the call.

88. Love yourself enough to **pay attention**

to the longings of your spirit; for the bridge to happiness that spans the chasm of life's irrelevance can only be discovered when you listen to your inner yearnings calling you to your destiny.

~♥~

MULTIMEDIA TRANSFORMATION

At times we can be so weighted down by guilt and sorrow over past mistakes of judgment and actions that before we can love ourselves we must forgive ourselves. Sometimes easier to say than to do. If you are burdened by the weight of past mistakes, my wife and I have created a two short, hypnotic affirmation, multimedia presentations to help you overcome your past and move on to your future. The URL address provided at the end of this chapter will lead you to the multimedia programs. There is one for **Forgiving Yourself** and another for **Loving Yourself**. These multimedia programs are intended to jump start your brain out of any old, destructive ruts and propel your thoughts and subsequently your actions onto new and beneficial paths.

1.The multimedia presentations will flash by

on your screen with images that last less than one second. Remember to blink normally as you view the multimedia presentation.

2. They will be accompanied by a simple music score, which you should listen to softly. It's repetitive score is part of the hypnotic effect of the multimedia. It's alright to turn the sound down quite softly if it helps you stay focused on the visual aspects, or even turn it off completely. If you have alternative calming and uplifting music you prefer, you can turn the sound off on the multimedia and play your own music in the background.

3. If you feel you have nothing to forgive yourself of then you can skip the Forgive Yourself multimedia. The reality is all of us have done and said things we should be sorry for and we may not have even admitted to ourselves yet that we need forgiveness, beginning with forgiving ourselves.

4. Watch the multimedia in privacy with no other sounds, people or pets in the room to distract you.

5. Watch each multimedia program twice a day for 7-10 minutes, with at least 1 hour between

viewings, for as many days as you feel you need until you see a dramatic difference in loving yourself. That said, don't watch the clock or use a timer. Stay focused on the multimedia and switch to the next phase when you feel it is right, based on the parameters that follow.

6. The first 2-3 minutes try to focus on the words without really noticing the pictures. Though the frames flash by quickly you can read the words if you focus.

7. The next 2-3 minutes, ignore the words and focus on making out the pictures as they flash by in each frame.

8. The next 3-4 minutes, ignore both the words and the pictures. Just stare at the center of the screen, remembering to blink from time to time. You should be seeing neither the pictures or words clearly. By staring at the screen without trying to discern either the pictures or the words your brain actually sees, records and reacts to both of them simultaneously.

9. Once through one 7-10 minute cycle you should repeat it at one other time in the day, ideally one in the morning shortly after arising, and the other viewing in the evening shortly

before retiring. If you are watching both Forgiving Yourself and Loving Yourself, you should wait at least 1 hour from finishing one before you watch the other. This allows your brain to meditate and process one long enough for the message to sink in deeply. But if that doesn't work in your hectic daily schedule you will still have immense benefit even if you watch one right after the other.

Copy and paste this URL into your browser's address bar,
http://kaleidoscope-publications.com/ Multimedia.html
to go now to the multimedia.

(Please be patient, the multi-media files contain high resolution pictures and audio. They may take 2-5 minutes to download depending upon your internet speed.)

~♥~

FINAL THOUGHTS

You are the master of your life either by commission or omission. If you choose to just accept whatever hand life deals you and however you feel about yourself good or bad, then you are the master by omission. Funny thing is, most people who are the masters of their life by omission don't feel at all like they are the masters. Just the opposite; they feel like they have no control. In reality, they don't have control. By just accepting whatever comes their way, they have voluntarily given up control of their own life. They are still the master of their life; however they made the choice to not take control. They are masters by omission.

Masters by commission on the other hand choose to take control of their life, at least in the important aspects. They commit to themselves and their future. They are motivated by the belief that they can make choices and take actions that will beneficially affect their lives in the ways they desire. Masters by commission are proactive in their own lives

Regardless of whether in your past you have been a master by commission or omission, by reading this book, meditating on the 88 reasons to love yourself, repeatedly watching the multimedia presentations, and daily affirming in the mirror and throughout your day that you love yourself, you will become the Master of your life. As you command, so it will be.

Go in your light, with love & joy,

Embrosewyn Tazkuvel

PS If you have enjoyed *Love Yourself*, I would be honored if you would take a few moments to revisit the book page on Amazon and leave a nice review.

~❤~

ABOUT THE AUTHOR

I have been blessed with some amazing experiences in my life that certainly have influenced me in the direction of wanting to help the people of the world. Many of my books penned under both Jesse Love and Embrosewyn Tazkuvel are written with that goal in mind. I've been fortunate to have traveled to many countries around the world and interacted with people from the president of the country to the family living in a shack with a dirt floor. Being among people of many cultures, religions and social standings, watching them in their daily lives, seeing their hopes and aspirations for their children and the joys they have with their families and friends, has continually struck me with a deep feeling of oneness. I've been with elderly people as they breathed their last breath and at the birth of babies when they take their first. It's all very humbling.

Love Yourself

This amazing world we live in and the wonderful people that fill it have given me so much. My books are my way to give back as much as I can to as many people as I can. Feel free to contact me through the contact form on *www.celestopea. com*.

~❤~

EMBROSEWYN'S BOOKS

WORDS OF POWER AND TRANSFORMATION
101+ Magickal Words and Sigils of Celestine
Light To Manifest Your Desires

Whatever you seek to achieve or change in your life, big or small, Celestine Light magickal words and sigils can help your sincere desires become reality.

Drawing from an ancient well of magickal power, the same divine source used by acclaimed sorcerers, witches and spiritual masters through the ages, the 101+ magickal words and sigils are revealed to the public for the very first time. They can create quick and often profound improvements in your life.

It doesn't matter what religion you follow or what you believe or do not believe. The magickal words and sigils are like mystical keys that open secret doors regardless of who holds the key. If you put the key in and turn it, the door will open and the magick will swirl around you!

From the beginner to the Adept, the Celestine Light words of power and sigils will expand your world and open up possibilities that may have seemed previously unachievable. Everything from something simple like finding a lost object, to something powerful like repelling a psychic or physical attack, to something of need such as greater income, to something life changing like finding your Soul Mate.

Some may wonder how a few spoken words combined with looking for just a moment at a peculiar image could have such immediate and often profound effects. The secret is these are ancient magick words of compelling power and the sigils are the embodiment of their magickal essence. Speaking or even thinking the words, or looking at or even picturing the sigil in your mind, rapidly draws angelic and magickal energies to you like iron to a magnet to fulfill the worthy purpose you desire.

This is a book of potent white magick of the light. Without a lot of training or ritual, it gives you the ability to overcome darkness threatening you from inside or out. For what is darkness except absence of the light? When light shines, darkness fades and disappears, not with a roar, but with a whimper.

Use the words and sigils to call in the magickal energies to transform and improve your life in every aspect. In this comprehensive book you will find activators to propel your personal growth, help you excel in school, succeed in your own business, or launch you to new heights in your profession. It will give you fast acting keys to improve your relationships, change your luck, revitalize your health, and develop and expand your psychic abilities.

Embrosewyn Tazkuvel is an Adept of the highest order in Celestine Light. After six decades of using magick and teaching it to others he is now sharing some of the secrets of what he knows with you. Knowledge that will instantly connect you to divine and powerful universal forces that with harmonic resonance, will unleash the magickal you!

Inside you will discover:

- 101 word combinations that call in magickal forces like a whirlwind of light.
- 177 magickal words in total.
- 101 sigils to go with each magickal word combination to amplify the magickal results you seek.
- 101 audio files you can listen to; helping you have perfect pronunciation of the Words of Power regardless of your native language. Available directly from the eBook and with a link in the paperback edition.

AURAS
How To See, Feel & Know

TOP REVIEWS

#1 Amazon bestseller in multiple categories since 2012. Used as a comprehensive reference book in aura and chakra classes around the world. Filled with real life accounts of Embrosewyns adventures with auras, plus 47 **full color** pictures and illustrations, with 17 dynamic eye exercises to help you rapidly begin to see the beautiful world of auras.

"Mr. Tazkuvel does a wonderful job at making such a complicated and specific subject like auras easy to learn while entertaining the reader with his own experiences as an aura reader throughout his life. The guide is well-written, casual but informative, vivid with imagery

(from pictures to illustrations), provides tips/tools for training the mind/eyes and ensures that the reader gets a comprehensive guide to auras in a real and tangible way."
~R. Coker, Amazon Top 1000 Reviewer

"This is one of the most interesting books I have read to date. I had absolutely no idea that I could 'train' myself to see auras! Although I still have a ways to go, I can honestly tell that I am able to pick up on people's auras. The parts on body language and the authors personal story were icing on the cake. Loved it and will definitely be telling everyone I know about it!" ~Momto4BookLover, Amazon Top 2000 Reviewer

"I was a huge skeptic and got the book thinking I was going to blast it in the reviews. After reading through it though I realize that I was completely wrong! The author does a great job explaining exactly what an aura is, as well as how to interpret them. There are very good exercises to help you train your eyes to see auras." ~Irish Times, Amazon Top 2000 Reviewer

Auras: How to See, Feel & Know, is like three books in one!

- It's an entertaining read as Embrosewyn recalls his early childhood and high school experiences seeing auras, and the often humorous reactions by everyone from his mother to his friends when he told them what he saw.
- It is also a complete training manual to help you quickly be able to see Auras in vibrant color. It includes

17 eye exercises and dozens of Full Color pictures, enabling anyone with vision in both eyes to begin seeing vividly colored auras around any person. The secret is in retraining the focusing parts of your eyes to see things that have always been there, but you have never been able to see before. Auras: How to See, Feel & Know, includes all the power techniques, tools and Full Color eye exercises from Embrosewyn's popular workshops.

• Additionally, there is a fascinating chapter on body language. Embrosewyn teaches in his workshops to not just rely on your interpretation of the aura alone, but to confirm it with another indicator such as body language. Auras: How to See, Feel & Know goes in depth with thorough explanations and great pictures to show you all the common body language indicators used to confirm what someone's aura is showing you.

For those who already have experience seeing auras, the deeper auric layers and subtle auric nuances and the special ways to focus your eyes to see them, are explained in detail, with accompanying Full Color pictures to show you how the deeper layers and auric aberrations appear.

SOUL MATE AURAS
How To Use Your Aura to Find Your Soul Mate

The romantic dream of finding your Soul Mate, the person with whom you resonate on every level of your being, is more than a wishful notion. It is a deeply embedded, primal desire that persists on some level despite what may have been years of quiet, inner frustration and included relationships that while fulfilling on some levels, still fell short of the completeness of a Soul Mate.

Once found, your relationship with your Soul Mate can almost seem like a dream at times. It will be all you expected and probably much more. Having never previously had a relationship that resonated in harmony and expansiveness on every level of your being, you will have had nothing to prepare you for its wonder. Having never stood atop a mountain that tall with an expansiveness so exhilarating, once experienced, a committed relationship with your Soul Mate will give you a bliss and fulfillment such as you probably only imagined in fairy tales.

But how to find your Soul Mate? That is the million dollar question. The vast majority of people believe finding your Soul Mate is like a magnetic attraction, it will somehow just happen; in some manner you'll just be inevitably drawn to each other. The harsh reality is, 99% of people realize by their old age that it never happened. Or, if it did occur they didn't recognize their Soul Mate at the time, because they were looking for a different ideal.

Soul Mate Auras: How to Use Your Aura to Find Your Soul Mate gives you the master keys to unlock the passageway to discovering your Soul Mate using the certainty of your auric connections. Every person has a unique aura and auric field generated by their seven energy centers and their vitality. Find the person that you resonate strongly with on all seven energy centers and you'll find your Soul Mate!

Everyone can sense and see auras. In Soul Mate Auras full color eye and energy exercises will help you learn how to see and feel auras and how to use that ability to identify where in the great big world your Soul Mate is living. Once you are physically in the presence of your prospective Soul Mate, you will know how to use your aura to energetically confirm that they are the one. The same methods can be used to discover multiple people that are Twin Flames with you; not quite seven auric connection Soul Mates, but still deep and expansive connections to you on five to six energy centers.

Soul Mate Auras also includes an in-depth procedure to determine if someone is a Twin Flame or Soul Mate, not by using your aura, but by honestly and rationally evaluating your connections on all seven of your energy centers. This is an invaluable tool for anyone contemplating marriage or entering a long-term committed relationship. It also serves as a useful second opinion confirmation for anyone that has used their aura to find their Soul Mate.

To help inspire and motivate you to create your own "happily ever after," Soul Mate Auras is richly accentuated with dozens of full color photos of loving couples along with profound quotes from famous to anonymous people about the wonder of Soul Mates.

Treat yourself to the reality of finding your Soul Mate or confirming the one that you have already found! Scroll to the upper left of the page and click on Look Inside to find out more about what's inside this book!

Secret Earth Series

INCEPTION
BOOK 1

TOP REVIEWS

"I simply couldn't put it down! It has, in some ways, changed the very way I think. It's exciting, adventurous and keeps you hanging on to the edge of your seat throughout! You don't wanna miss this one!" ~**Barbara Cary, Amazon Top 1000 Reviewer**

"The writing is clear and vivid, both opening doors in readers' imaginations and making heady concepts accessible at the same time." ~**Alex Prosper, Amazon Top 1000 Reviewer**

"What an adventurous and mind-captivating story! I absolutely loved it! If you are like me, you will find yourself not being able to put this book down until it is finished. That's how good it is. I could easily see it being made into a full-scale Hollywood movie." ~**Anna , Amazon Top 5000 Reviewer**

Could it be possible that there is a man alive on the Earth today that has been here for two thousand years? How has he lived so long? And why? What secrets does he know? Can his knowledge save the Earth or is it doomed?

Continuing the epic historical saga begun in the *Oracles of Celestine Light*, but written as a novel rather than a chronicle, Inception unveils the life and adventures of Lazarus of Bethany and his powerful and mysterious sister Miriam of Magdala.

The first book of the Secret Earth series, *Inception*, reveals the hidden beginnings of the strange, secret life of Lazarus. From his comfortable position as the master of caravans to Egypt he is swept into a web of intrigue involving his enigmatic sister Miriam and a myriad of challenging dangers that never seem to end and spans both space and time.

Some say Miriam is an angel, while others are vehement that she is a witch. Lazarus learns the improbable truth about his sister, and along with twenty-three other courageous men and women, is endowed with the secrets of immortality. But he learns that living the secrets is not as easy as knowing them. And living them comes at a price; one that needs to be paid in unwavering courage, stained with blood, built with toil, and endured with millenniums of sacrifice, defending the Earth from all the horrors that might have been. Inception is just the beginning of their odyssey.

DESTINY
BOOK 2

In preparation, before beginning their training as immortal Guardians of the Earth, Lazarus of Bethany and his wife Hannah were asked to go on a short visit to a world in another dimension. "Just to look around a bit and get a feel for the differences," Lazarus's mysterious sister, Miriam of Magdala assured them.

She neglected to mention the ravenous monstrous birds, the ferocious fire-breathing dragons, the impossibly perfect people with sinister ulterior motives, and the fact that they would end up being naked almost all the time! And that was just the beginning of the challenges!

UNLEASH YOUR PSYCHIC POWERS

TOP REVIEWS

"Along with information on auras, channeling and animal whispering it contains just about every psychic and paranormal topic you can think of. The section on Ki energy was also very good- make that excellent. The author really over delivers in material and it is a nice change from books with hardly any info." ~**Diana L., Amazon Top 500 Reviewer**

"The author shows a skill for weaving words and explaining the intricacies of the wealth of psychic realms, managing to introduce me to all the many psychic areas a person could become proficient in... and then he showed me how to begin my journey of uncovering my own talents in the psychic world. From a reader's standpoint, the book is filled with countless insights into psychic powers/abilities as well as a deeper understanding of how to train your mind/body to become in tune with the psychic world." ~**L. Collins, Amazon Top 1000 Reviewer**

"A welcome relief. I was a little skeptical about the validity of the contents of this book . . . UNTIL I read it. Being a paranormal researcher myself, and up-to-date on psychic phenomena, the ins and outs, the dos and don'ts, and all the scams in-between, I was ready for a none too favorable review. How nice to be disappointed! This impressive book is very well written; and remarkably - it is comprehensive

without being boring. I strongly suggest that you read it from cover to cover BEFORE delving into the supernatural world of Psychic Power - from Channeling to Psychic Self Defense, and Telepathy to my personal favorite- Lucid Dreams." ~Lyn Murray, **Author-Poet Laureate-Artist**

A comprehensive guidebook for all levels of practitioners of the psychic and paranormal arts. Each one of the twenty supernatural abilities presented, including Clairvoyance, Animal Whispering, Lucid Dreaming, Precognition, Astral Projection, Channeling, Telekinesis and Telepathy, include easy-to-follow, step-by-step instructions on how you can unleash the full potential of these potent powers in your own life. Spiced with personal stories of Embrosewyn's five decades of experience discovering, developing and using psychic and paranormal talents. Paranormal abilities have saved Embrosewyn's life and the lives of his family members on multiple occasions. Learning to fully develop your own supernatural talents may come in just as handy one day.

PSYCHIC SELF DEFENSE

TOP REVIEW

Regardless of your beliefs, its an elegantly composed and greatly fascinating book. The writer's composing style easy is to follow through. I've read a couple of pages I ended up unable to put the book down. Assuming that you've generally been fascinated about whether psychic capabilities are "genuine" or perhaps that you have some of your own, this is really the book that you need to peruse. ~Jayden Sanders, **Amazon Top 10,000 Reviewer**

Have you ever felt a negative energy come over you for no apparent reason when you are near someone or around certain places? Psychic Self Defense details 17 common psychic threats, with exact, effective counter measures including many real life examples from Embrosewyn's 5 decades of personal experiences with the paranormal, devising what works and what doesn't from hard won trial and error.

Both the neophyte and the experienced will find a wealth of specific how-to methods to counter all forms of psychic attacks: from projections of negative thoughts from other people, to black magic curses, to hauntings by disembodied spirits, to energy sucking vampires, or attacks by demons.

Psychic Self Defense should be in the library of every psychic and serious student of the paranormal, and absolutely read by every medium, channeler, or person who makes any contact with forces, entities, or beings from the world beyond.

Psychic Self Defense is also available as an AUDIO BOOK.

22 STEPS TO THE LIGHT OF YOUR SOUL

TOP REVIEWS

This is a beautiful book. The word "generous" comes to mind. It's presented in such a way that you don't need to retain or absorb a whole lot of information at once - you can just dip into certain parts, and save others for later... so good. It opened my imagination and set my spirit spinning with possibilities and ideas. It's rare to find a book with this effect. The authors writing grabbed me from the get-go; it's charming, smooth, and intelligent without being pretentious. An amazing read. ~**Holly Wood, Amazon Top 4000 Reviewer**

There is something at work when you read the pages of this book. It feels like you are reading a dream. Not a scary dream, yet a dream where you are a little on edge. In this intimate book, the author shares with you his journey and the knowledge he has unlocked. The dream like feeling is maybe your mind awakening. I have read many of these new-age books during the past year. I can tell you that this is more advanced than many. It is challenging if you are new on your journey, yet it is fulfilling. 5/5 stars. ~**G. McFadden, Amazon Top 12,000 Reviewer**

What would it be like if you could reach through space and time to query the accumulated wisdom of the ages and get an answer to the mist vexing questions in your own life? ***22 Steps to the Light of Your Soul*** reveals such treasured insights, eloquently expounding upon the foundational principles of 22 timeless subjects of universal interest and appeal, to help each reader grow and expand into their fullest potential.

In a thought-provoking, poetic writing style, answers to questions we all ponder upon, such as love, happiness, success and friendship, are explored and illuminated in short, concise chapters, perfect for a thought to ponder through the day or contemplate as your eyes close for sleep.

Each paragraph tells a story and virtually every sentence could stand alone as an inspiring quote on your wall.

22 Steps to the Light of Your Soul is also available as an
AUDIO BOOK.

ORACLES OF CELESTINE LIGHT
Complete Trilogy Of Genesis, Nexus & Vivus

TOP REVIEWS

*I I have never read a book more touching and enlightening
as this Trilogy of books! This book is for anyone searching
for truth in whatever form or place it may be found. It will
resonate with you to your very soul if have an open mind
to see it. This is what I have been searching for, the missing
pieces to the puzzle, the mysteries, the deeper teachings of
Yeshua. Thank you so much for sharing this treasure with
the world, my life is ever enriched because of it!* ~**Jamie,
Amazon Top 1000 Reviewer**

*ts hard to describe, but reading the details of the garden
of Eden, to Adam and Eve, to their banishment, was more
complete and plausible than anything the bible states. For
starters, it wasn't just Adam and Eve, but 12 men and 12
woman, and from them they built up the human race in
the garden, and were called Edenites. This is just a small
taste of the astounding history that fills in the gaps that the
bible has. This book, especially for the very religious, might
be hard to read, but I implore you to give it an open mind.
You might just find your entire world, and spiritual view,
will be opened up.* ~**Jamie, Amazon Top 1000 Reviewer**

The controversial Oracles of Celestine Light, is a portal
in time to the days of Yeshua of Nazareth, over 2000
years ago, revealed in fulfilling detail to the world by the

reclusive Embrosewyn Tazkuvel. It includes 155 chapters of sacred wisdom, miracles and mysteries revealing life-changing knowledge about health, longevity, happiness and spiritual expansion that reverberates into your life today.

Learn the startling, never before understood truth about: aliens, other dimensions, Atlantis, Adam & Eve, the Garden of Eden, Noah and the ark, giants, the empowerment of women, dreams, angels, Yeshua of Nazareth (Jesus), his crucifixion & resurrection, his wife Miriam of Magdala (Mary Magdala), Yudas Iscariot (Judas), the afterlife, reincarnation, energy vortexes, witches, magic, miracles, paranormal abilities, and you!

The Oracles of Celestine Light turns accepted religious history and traditional teachings on their head. But page by page, it makes more sense than anything you've ever read and shares simple yet profound truths to make your life better today and help you to understand and unleash your miraculous potential.

The Oracles of Celestine Light explains who you are, why you are here, and your divine destiny. It is a must-read for anyone interested in spirituality, personal growth and thought-provoking answers to the unknown. Unknown

Psychic Awakening Series
CLAIRVOYANCE
BOOK 1

TOP REVIEW

For those who don't know what Clairvoyance is, check this

book out and learn. Even if you don't believe it, read it anyway. I learned quite a bit more than I originally knew about it. Check it out! ~**Cayce Hrivnak, Amazon Top 15,000 Reviewer**

Would it be helpful to you if you could gain hidden knowledge about a person, place, thing, event, or concept, not by any of your five physical senses, but with visions and "knowing?" ***Clairvoyance*** takes you on a quest of self-discovery and empowerment, helping you unlock this potent ability in your life. It includes riveting personal stories from Embrosewyn's six decades of psychic and paranormal adventures, plus fascinating accounts of others as they discovered and cultivated their supernatural abilities.

Clearly written, step-by-step practice exercises will help you to expand and benefit from your own clairvoyant abilities. This can make a HUGE improvement in your relationships, career and creativity. As Embrosewyn has proven from over twenty years helping thousands of students to find and develop their psychic and paranormal abilities, EVERYONE, has one or more supernatural gifts. ***Clairvoyance*** will help you discover and unleash yours!

TELEKINESIS
BOOK 2

TOP REVIEWS

Telekinesis is a great read. The author is a gifted storyteller and his personal experiences and journey are captivating and give some nice insight into focusing. The best parts of the book are how much time is spent on the different exercises and experiments that are here to help you practice and expand your abilities. ~**D Roberts, Amazon Top 6000 Reviewer**

This author does an excellent job of describing events that have happened to him and others pertaining to telekinesis. He also gives an outstanding explanation of what it actually is and how it works. I believe that anyone that is interested in harnessing this ability should take the time to read this fantastic book and learn from someone who has actually had these experiences himself. ~**L. Harrison, Amazon Top 10,000 Reviewer**

Telekinesis, also known as psychokinesis, is the ability to move or influence the properties of objects without physical contact. Typically it is ascribed as a power of the mind. But as Embrosewyn explains, based upon his 5 decades of personal experience, the actual physical force that moves and influences objects emanates from a person's auric field. It initiates with a mental thought, but the secret to the power is in your aura!

This book is filled with proven, exercises and training techniques to help you unlock this formidable paranormal ability. Spiced with accounts of real-life experiences by both Embrosewyn and others, you'll be entertained while you learn. But along the way you will begin to unleash the potent power of *Telekinesis* in your own life!

DREAMS
BOOK 3

TOP REVIEW

Spellbound with this book. A fantastic and informative read. ~ **Brandy**

In **Dreams**, renowned psychic/paranormal practitioner Embrosewyn Tazkuvel reveals some of his personal experiences with the transformational effect of dreams, while sharing time-tested techniques and insights that will help you unlock the power of your own night travels.

An expanded section on Lucid Dreaming gives you proven methods to induce and expand your innate ability to control your dreams. It explores the astonishing hidden world of your dream state that can reveal higher knowledge, greatly boost your creativity, improve your memory, and help you solve vexing problems of everyday life that previously seemed to have no solution.

Detailing the nine types of dreams will help you to understand which dreams are irrelevant and which you should pay close attention to, especially when they reoccur. You'll gain insight into how to interpret the various types of dreams to understand which are warnings of caution, and which are gems of inspiration that can change your life from the moment you awaken and begin to act upon that which you dreamed.

Dreaming while you sleep is a part of your daily life and cumulatively it accounts for dozens of years of your total life. It is a valuable time of far more than just rest. Become the master of your dreams and your entire life can become more than you ever imagined possible. Your dreams are the secret key to your future.

A Note From Embrosewyn About Your Soul Name

As many people who have read my books or attended my seminars over the years are aware, one of the things I use my psychic gifts for is to discover a person's Soul Name. Knowing this name and the meaning and powers of the sounds has proven to be transformational in the lives of some people. It has always been a great privilege for me to be asked to find a Soul Name for someone. But as my books have become more popular and numerous over the years, with new titles actively in the works in both the *Secret Earth series* and the *Awakening Psychic series*, plus sequels to popular stand alone books such as *Auras*, I have less and less time available to discover a Soul Name for someone when they request it. Doing so requires up to 2 hours of uninterrupted meditation time, which is a fairly great challenge for me to find these days.

With these time constraints in mind, it will generally be five to seven days once I receive your picture before I can get back to you with your Soul Name. I do hope everyone will understand. If you would like to know more about Soul Names please visit this site, *www.mysoulname.com*.

Namaste,

Embrosewyn

Before you go...one last thing

If you have enjoyed *Love Yourself*, I would be honored if you would take a few moments to revisit the book page on Amazon and leave a nice review. Thank you!

Made in the USA
Middletown, DE
04 January 2017